Honeysuckle

poems by

Robin Gow

Finishing Line Press
Georgetown, Kentucky

Honeysuckle

Copyright © 2019 by Robin Gow
ISBN 978-1-64662-097-5 First Edition
All rights reserved under International and Pan-American Copyright Conventions. No part of this book may be reproduced in any manner whatsoever without written permission from the publisher, except in the case of brief quotations embodied in critical articles and reviews.

ACKNOWLEDGMENTS

Penn Review "Intravenous Therapy" May 2019

Lackadaisy "I'll name myself honeysuckle" Summer 2019

Publisher: Leah Maines

Editor: Christen Kincaid

Cover Art: Robin Gow

Author Photo: Robin Gow

Cover Design: Elizabeth Maines McCleavy

Printed in the USA on acid-free paper.
Order online: www.finishinglinepress.com
        also available on amazon.com

                Author inquiries and mail orders:
                      Finishing Line Press
                      P. O. Box 1626
                Georgetown, Kentucky 40324
                         U. S. A.

Table of Contents

I'll name myself honeysuckle 1

small town, what would you like? 3

Shelling 4

Aubade to my father 7

Frozen Dinner Family 9

& a web grows in my mouth 10

Communion 12

Institut für Sexualwissenschaft (1919-1923) 13

Sometimes I have nightmares/dreams my Grindr date will turn

    into a policeman 18

Intravenous Therapy 20

In the Artic a 300-Year-Old Greenland Shark Talks to Divers 23

I'll name myself honeysuckle

        to trade places
with the bush up the street from my house.

The bush can be *Sarah*
        be a girl with skin for ticks
to plunge
their heads in when she spends
too long picking
        sweet white yellow flowers
with her mom.

I'll name myself *honeysuckle*
because the bush
        has a thousand faces
all of them
bursting
                some of them dried
        fallen into green tangle.

Because the bush doesn't
have a mom to name it
        or hold its myriad hands
while it grows
becoming strange
even to itself
        becoming a home for ants
and gnats and ticks and bees.

I'll name myself *honeysuckle*
because sometimes all we have
is metaphor
        to name a desire.

            I raise myself
on a series of symbols

a notebook full of words I wish
I could use as a name:
        ivy
        vine
        onion
        dandelion

I'm here climbing
        into the honeysuckle bush

        sticky with the syrup
from spilling flower cups.

Not a girl name.
Not a boy name.

        And Mom would walk
        here with Sarah
and I would not
have to be her.

She and Mom
        would pluck flowers.
        Drink fragments of me.

I would feel the insects moving
across all my limbs with
        no need to fear blood
or body: strange with growing.

small town, what would you like?

i'm thinking
of the diner
in my hometown.
everyone has a diner.
everyone has a hometown.
i say,
i want everything on the menu!
thank you. yes.
i say,
bring me plate by plate!
i need it all,
every single dish
because i'm american!
i'm thinking of the diner!
in my hometown! everyone! has a diner
hometown! a clatter! of white!! heavy! plates: faces
to pile! with egg! ooze! toast triangles! square packets of
grape jelly! see it all piled!!! around me!!! a booth seat! tear! in the red! cushion by the window! with guests peering in! i'm not eating! any of it! just need to watch! index! finger! pointing! count every single! egg to make sure! none are missing! yellow chicken! souls! scrapple! bacon! ham! i don't eat meat!! i just watch! asking each to turn! back into an animal! pigs!!! standing on the table!! ordering more!!! coffee! bottomless! coffee! pouring from! a cup! pouring over my head! need take out boxes!!! take everything home! but not! before gazing!! glisten! hash!-brown! crackle spam! pucker! pancake!! melt!-ing!! butter!!! eye eating! praising! just!! me!!! all just me!!!!! fork! in! mouth! all mine all mine!!!! all mine!!!! all mine!!!! all mine!!!! all mine!!!! all mine!!!!!!!!!!!!!!!!!

Shelling

1.
Mom pinches
the edamame pod's small stem
twisting till the green pocket comes free
Plink in the metal bowl on the ground
nestled between our matching callous feet
I find an ant on my thigh
and I smash its small form
brushing away the smudge

2.
A bucket of KFC chicken
perches on the dining room table at our great aunt's
grease stains making strange shapes on package
Dad pours the legs out in a plate passing
the warm-bottom dish around I take a wing
and pick at the copper-color skin to find
the white flesh beneath placing the meat into my mouth
just to spit a piece of sinew into a paper napkin

3.
By the side of the creek
we three wandered eight-grade girls
gone ambling in the brush towards
the water shooing away
a cloud of gnats when a rat snake
slick and ink thrashed between
our bare feet
belly smooth over the tips of my toes

4.
A great white python
held up by two zookeepers
in a room full of second graders
The animal's red eyes all scarlet
like my birth stone I thought *July*
I imagined that if the snake wanted to it could decide
to devour the people holding it and then still not full turn to us kids
we'd be lumps in its stomach like podded peas

5.
When I drive
sometimes I think about
veering off into traffic
Not by accident
on purpose
How by gripping the wheel and spinning
I could smash car after car
mess of glass and metal

6.
In middle school
I would make roses
out of aluminum foil
I had a whole assembly line
at the kitchen counter
used up roll after roll of foil
put the roses in vases for when
Mom came home from work

7.
They said to check your canoe
for snakes I found none but
did end up smashing a thick coarse-hair spider
under my shoe The tall trees of the pine barrens
peered down at us and our flimsy rafts
as my biology class readied for a day on the copper-water river
Most canoes seated pair so I felt lucky to go alone
envisioning my own capsize a bean slipping out of the pod

8.
I don't know what the small white flowers
that grew in our front yard are called
I picked them
holding their soft faces
carrying them to the kitchen where
I'd float their visages in mason jars
imagining each as life raft
that I would step out onto if I could

Aubade to my father who leaves for work at the battery factory by 3:40am everyday

This morning I think of tucking you into a daffodil bell
and sealing closed the mouth of the flower
so that you can sleep in past 4am for once.

Inside there, the sun would be even more yellow
on your face as it woke you. Maybe you would
take your time with breakfast for once, chewing,

butterfly-like, the yolky pollen caked on each stamen,
instead of standing at the breakfast counter,
eating handfuls of dry cheerios from the bag

and sipping Diet Coke, the fizz, prickly as it mixes
with cereal. You would have to wait for me
to release you from the petals and I would wait

till late afternoon, till the whole day was as
good as spent. Maybe with all that time to yourself
you would give into a nap or two, you would

touch the pistol, the flower's female heart
throbbing with life and something would shift
in you and you'd decide to never return to the factory.

This would be cruel then, because we both know
that you have to go to the factory, that you
have to watch batteries as they crawl down

the conveyor belt, have to clip their wires in place,
each wire thin as the necks of the daffodil
I want to hide you in. Dad, I want to plant daffodils

inside your sunken mattress, weight of your body
worn into that valley where you never sleep enough.
I want to fill that valley with soil, I want you to skip

work. I want to go to the factory, and build
all your batteries for you, but here I am with the daffodils,
planning an impossible escape.

Frozen Dinner Family

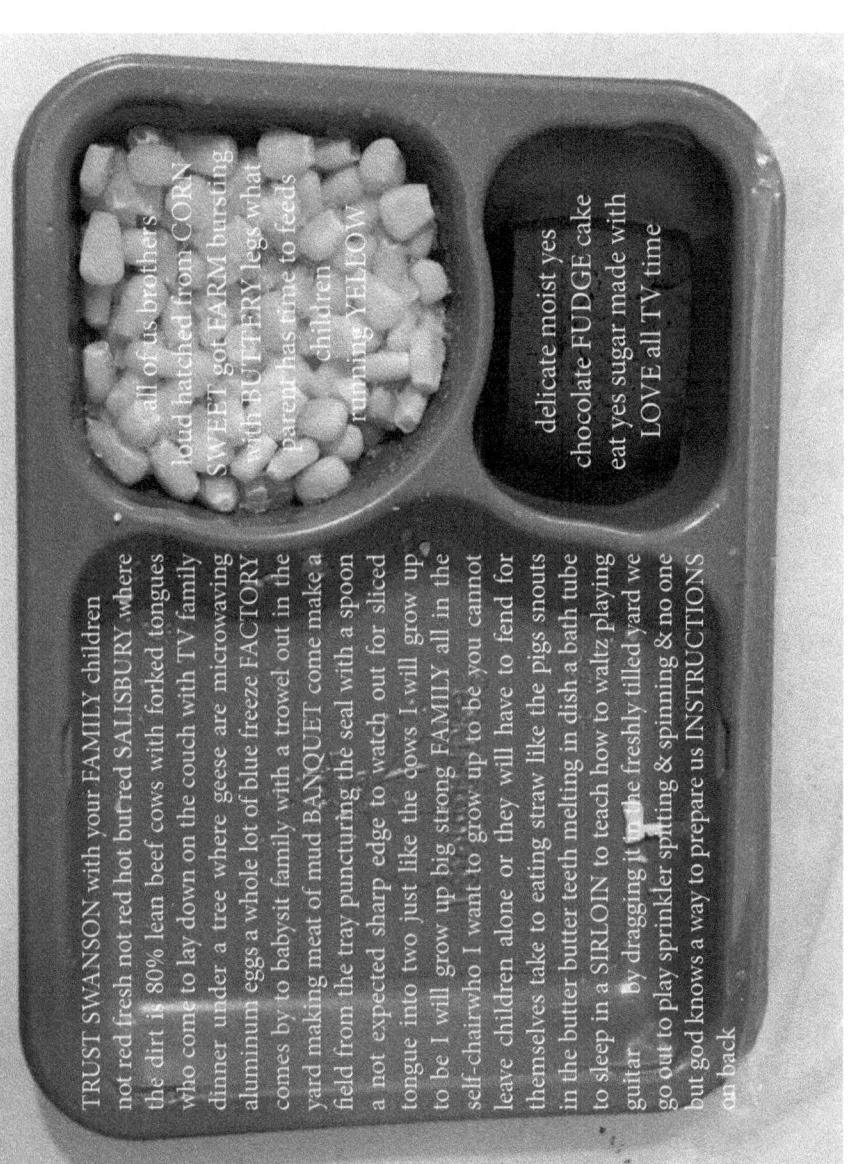

Corn compartment: all of us brothers loud hatched from CORN SWEET got FARM bursting with BUTTERY legs what parent has time to feeds children running YELLOW

Cake compartment: delicate moist yes chocolate FUDGE cake eat yes sugar made with LOVE all TV time

Main compartment: TRUST SWANSON with your FAMILY children not red fresh not red hot but red SALISBURY where the dirt is 80% lean beef cows with forked tongues who come to lay down on the couch with TV family dinner under a tree where geese are microwaving aluminum eggs a whole lot of blue freeze FACTORY comes by to babysit family with a trowel out in the yard making meat of mud BANQUET come make a field from the tray puncturing the seal with a spoon a not expected sharp edge to watch out for sliced tongue into two just like the cows I will grow up to be I will grow up big strong FAMILY all in the self-chairwho I want to grow up to be you cannot leave children alone or they will have to fend for themselves take to eating straw like the pigs snouts in the butter butter teeth melting in dish a bath tube to sleep in a SIRLOIN to teach how to waltz playing guitar by dragging it up the freshly tilled yard we go out to play sprinkler spitting & spinning & no one but god knows a way to prepare us INSTRUCTIONS on back

& a web grows in my mouth

each night
& i don't tell you
& i spit it out in the sink
& it's all wet fine white strings like veins of a dead instrument
& sometimes there's beetles from the web i spit out too
& flies
& flecks of moth wing

& do you remember when you taught me to feed moths to spiders?
& how that was a lie
& it was really me
& i showed you how
& i cupped my hands in the porch lights
& trapped the fluttering insects
&& i hate moths
& the dust that comes off their wings
& when they're scared
& i feel them, desperate in my cage
& call them "paper heart"
& "bowl of eyelashes"

& i know all this is cruel now, but in the moment there was a certain rush of life
& that come from when you feed one animal to another
& i imagine it's the same for people who drop rats into snake cages
& you handle me like a moth
& put a finger on my bra strap
& a finger in my hair
& i catch the moths
& they have sandy brown wings
& i have practiced the art of letting you make a moth of me
& i don't know how to not be a moth

& once you caught a moth with white wings
& marvelous green eyes
& asked me if it was too big for the spiders
& i said "no"
& you tossed the moth like a baby bird right into the tangle
& we watched side by side
& it was romantic, the spider struggling to wrap the huge moth
& the moth was staring at us, as if we were its parents
& the moth was asking us aloud what it had done wrong
& the spider encircled its body with more bondage

& i had flinched
& scratched my arm
& i had wanted, in that moment, to intervene
& free her

i imagined sticking my
hand in, pulling the mouth out
how grateful she would be
the moth wobbling at first
wings still sticky from the web
i would hold her till she re-learned how to
pulse her wings
my paper paper heart
my bowl of eye lashes
we would grow old together
on the porch
without you

Communion

With a knife, he draws circles on my arm.
I lay down with Jesus in a greased pan
asking how long he works his flesh with harm
to have enough skin for Sunday; one-man

becoming unleavened petals. I kiss
him on the neck. He tastes wet; needs more salt.
Preheat oven. Olive oil abyss
where I can tell him that it was my fault

I dropped him on the white floor of the church.
"I don't want you to forgive me," I say,
as he feeds me host after host, each perch
& turn to doves in my teeth. "Lord come splay

me wide open," I plea as he teases
with the knife's dull side. "Tear me to pieces."

Institut für Sexualwissenschaft (1919-1932)

Dear Magnus Hirschfield,

I.
I'm planning an escape
to your Institute for Sexual Science.
I pack all my things
into two bags:
one for clothes, one for books.
I place them by the
front door and

early morning, I slip
out and down the street,
each sidewalk square, a decade,
until I reach 1919, Berlin.

II.
Your Institute is the only building in the whole city,
surrounded by trees even taller, their branches mixing with clouds.
I consider taking a picture outside,
but I realize my phone has turned into a stone.

I could never find photographs of the place
as I'd search late into the night on websites
all written in German.
[click TRANSLATE]

III.
This is a different history
one untouched by *forward*
(which I've learned doesn't always mean better).

I knock and the great huge wooden doors
open on their own
the wings of a carved bird.

IV.
Inside the walls are made of books,
their spins all ordered alphabetical.
I spend ten years just reading
each title aloud so that they echo down
vast hallways.
I imagine you placing each one
with the help of your partners.

V.
There's a sitting room where tall women sit
smoking with skinny black cigarette holders,
the smog coming out in morphing colors:
blue to pink to blue to purple.
One with a red feather boa asks, "Who are you?"
a deep fuchsia cloud pouring from her mouth.

I say, "I'm Robin" and
she laughs, "What a lovely name!"
as she pulls a robin out of her boa,
handing the bird to me.
I let it perch on my finger.

Another, wearing silk gloves, asks,
"Are you a transsexual?"
Her fingers are
light, watching them is like
witnessing a piano
play itself.

I say, "I am, that's why I'm here,"
so they flock around me, sit me on their velvet deep purple couches
and tell me, "You must never leave"
and "This is the only place where we can be ourselves."

VI.
They say if everyone stays in here
time won't move, that we can pin
time down,
that time can belong
to us and we can
stay here alone together
where everything's safe.

I ask, "Is it really safe here?"
and the robin chirps.
The women admonish the bird, they say, "Hush!"

VII.
I move on, carrying the bird
as their chatter sounds dampen.

I tell the creature to take me to you
and it flies so fast that I have to run after it.

I sprint down hall after hall,
past homosexual men arm in arm
and trans men teaching each other how to bind their chests,
past women planting violets in each other's hair
and people in striped gender-ambiguous bathing suits.

VIII.
Your office has glass doors,
the bird pries them open with its beak.

The bird
asks, "Are you sure you want to see?"

And I say, "I do,
I do."

I step inside and almost fall
into the great pit;
a wound
dug into the soil,

a grave dug so deep
there is no bottom.

Far below I notice bodies still falling,
and I suppose they plummeted weeks ago.

"You told me it was safe," I say

and bird says, "You asked to see,
you asked to see."

IX.
For a second, I think I should fall in,
let my body be
swallowed up with the others.

Then I think
of you and
the hole your body makes in me.

X.
I will never know what your
Institute was really like.

Alone, I read articles through the night.

They tell me you took
care of transsexual people,
that you wanted to protect them,
and, maybe, by extension
that you wanted
to protect me.

Is my imagining
another kind of
forgetting?

Sometimes I have nightmares/dreams my Grindr date will turn into a policeman

We'll meet discrete.
No profile—picture no name
for either of us
just our Grindr gray silhouettes

and my profile might as well be
the profile of a shore bird:
a plover, a sandpiper
with all their flushing and
all their eager worry.

Exchange body for body
and he'll be one of those guys
who says he's "not gay"
just wants to fuck men;
just wants
to fuck me.

But then he'll cum
blooming oil
navy blue
from his cock and I will
have known
        this would happen all along,

one would be a policeman
spilling
his glorious uniform
all the black/blue
a separated bruise
the sunglasses dripping
staining my feathers.

Wings pinned down on the bed;
a twitch of knees
an urge to break.

This will happen because
pollution requires water.
Him throbbing
with uncontainable need.

I'll shut my eyes
and imagine the oil spill
in the Gulf of Mexico
and how he, like an oil tanker,
can hold nothing
but the potential for rupture.
What can his body do
but spill onto me
with all that horror?

See: photographs of birds
drenched in oil
so deep they
become oil.

I'll be
the flammable animal.

This fuel is fossil:
a loud rotting.

But, after we're done,
I will be thankful
he came because
I'll no longer be waiting
for our inevitable encounter.

       I'll molt in the shower after,
oil swirling
grime feathers
clogging drain.

Intravenous Therapy

i ask the needle
to be my mother or
at least an ocean while
i focus on you in the corner
of the hospital room
you say *it'll be over quick*
as you turn to water
a cold
salt wave behind my eyes
i've never been to the Arctic
but it sounds
wild
wet
i imagine
that's where my great great great
grandmothers carved each other
out of hunks of ice
a necklace of pearls
a beach made of flurry
made of frozen fruit washing
up on the shore
the nurse fills
the IV bag with the entire
Arctic ocean
tells me i need to
take it all in
drip by drip. january sun enters
my blood walking on frost-bitten
bare feet
maroon cold-burnt skin
all the pieces
of fruit are unripe purple-blue
i hold them up high
asking god to do
his magic
make them sweet

turn them into mothers
when i was small i would dare
myself to eat the skin off
unripe plums bitter scabs
i toss their pits into
the ocean
plum trees grow
underwater
roots digging into ice
in search of the grandmothers
i feel the pits
crawling through the tube
like beetles marching
into my blood, planting themselves
somewhere deep i open my mouth
so they will have sun
so they might melt
i ask you what those things are called
that keep time
you say *an hourglass?*
i say *yes, an hour glass.*
the nurse sets an hourglass
on the windowsill
says *this is how long you have left*
it doesn't seem very long
i think my hourglass is filled with
snow not sand.
our family tree
a plum tree growing inside an iceberg
the fruits washing up
on shore were all
my popsicle people
one of them probably my mother
where is she today?
the nurse says *generally family comes*
along for things like this

so you come sit by me
you watch as i
crawl deeper into the ocean
the Arctic
everything quiet
just my great great great
grandmothers stirring
the ocean with all their purple hands
in the water. i have little desire
to travel now that i can feel
the whole ocean inside me
i invite you inside too,
collect pearls collect ice
you squeeze my hand
i plea
feed me plums

In the Artic a 300-Year-Old Greenland Shark Talks to Divers

      describe me
I want to know
      what language I make in you
sound too fast to be alive
    ink child
      eyes   sky cut
   how deep do
you go today?

     have you known
edge ending blue
like offspring who've fallen
      from my body
in their soft worlds
     sphere oceans
each current
     tide heart muscle ripping

I have never met
one of them
     what do you call
the pieces of your body
when they
     stray off?

     our kind pass
each other like icebergs breaking
      falling from cloud
no language but blue deep
     hollow hum
between bodies
I want to collide
     collide blue hard

what ocean dangles
        up there?
        I name
        the great angry glimmer
        "Mother"
tell myself
        how that white glow
must have asked
my hatching
        must have touched
something hard enough
        to make another
        and another
        and another

I want all your speaking
            speak at me
            in me
do you love your making mouth
or is it all cold
talk to me blue
        with green intentions
I am older than older
        than whatever limbs
        you move

        if I tried on your
bodies I'd climb
so far that time
        would leak
I would die in color

I would enter the higher ocean
thin water eating me
       I would tell
Mother I am alive
I know her
       I too
have made creatures
just to watch them
sink

Robin Gow lives in Mineola, NY with his partner, his friends, and his dog Gertrude. He writes a poem every morning before he takes a run. His poetry has recently received awards from Brooklyn Poets, Negative Capability Press, Brain Mill Press, and Fearsome Creatures. His chapbook *A Museum for That Which No Longer Exists* was runner up for New Delta Review's Chapbook competition and his chapbook *Some Metaphors Are Self-Inflicted* was runner up for Glass Poetry's Chapbook flash reading period. He is the editor at large for *Village of Crickets* and social media coordinator for *Oyster River Pages*. He is an out and proud bisexual transgender man passionate about LGBT issues and he has given LGBT inclusivity trainings at universities and health care networks across the country. When he's not writing poetry he also loves baking and reading about Octopuses.

www.ingramcontent.com/pod-product-compliance
Lightning Source LLC
LaVergne TN
LVHW041312080426
835510LV00009B/965